Greta's

Greta Rado

Greta's Story

A Memoir

Shane
best wishes
Greta

Greta's Story: A Memoir
ISBN 978 1 74027 493 7
Copyright © Greta Rado 2008

First published 2008 by
GINNINDERRA PRESS
79B Lipson Street Port Adelaide SA 5015

Printed by Pirion Digital, Fyshwick, ACT

Contents

I dedicate this book to the memory of my daughter, Susi, and to my two granddaughters, Linda and Elizabeth.

I would also like to thank Jenny Horsfield; without her help and encouragement I would never have written this book.

Editor's Introduction

When I was a schoolgirl in North Sydney in the 1960s, my friends were the daughters of Jewish refugees from Poland, Czechoslovakia and Hungary. These people had managed to escape from the chaos and misery of post-war Europe and with intelligence and hard work had won for themselves a degree of prosperity and security in their new homeland.

My closest friend, Susi Rado, was the only child of two such refugees, Andrew Rado, a Hungarian, and his Austrian wife, Greta. This young couple had lived through the Nazi occupation in Hungary, losing many of their relatives at Auschwitz or by deportation to other camps. Their own survival is still a source of wonder to them. They married in Budapest early in 1946 and Susi was born a year later. Their decision to escape from Russian-occupied Hungary in 1948 and emigrate to Australia was part of the story Susi had shared with me about her early childhood. By the time I met her, Susi's parents had established a successful import business and were part of Sydney's large Hungarian émigré community. Their home, overlooking Middle Harbour, intrigued me with its beautiful collection of ceramics, rugs and paintings, expressions of a culture so very different from that I was familiar with.

Susi had hoped some day to write down the remarkable story of her parents' lives. She was never given that opportunity, struck down with breast cancer in her forties.

Her two children, Linda and Elizabeth, were too young when their mother died to fully appreciate their grandparents' history. Now they are both young adults and it is for them, primarily, that this story is written.

I am honoured that Greta Rado has entrusted me with the task of transcribing her memories, which she recorded on tape over a number of months in 2007. The reader will find that her memory is sharp and her own, eloquent voice comes through clearly in this oral history.

The Holocaust has had many interpreters. Its survivors all have their own stories of pain, loss and courage. Greta's story can now be added to that collection.

Jennifer Horsfield
February 2008

Part One

Margit Goldschmied was born in a private clinic on 8 February 1921 in Vienna, two and a half years after the end of the First World War. Her parents were Isidor and Frieda Goldschmied. This is Margit's story...or Greta's story, as this as what she was always called.

Before my sister was born, I was an only child and very spoilt. My parents lived in a nice, big apartment in Vienna, very comfortable, only ten minutes walk from the Opera.

Greta with her parents, Vienna, 1921.

Greta with nurse, 1921.

My father was a wealthy coffee merchant. He had been born into the Austro-Hungarian Empire, and was a clever, humorous man, with a good grasp of languages: he spoke German, Hungarian and Italian perfectly.

There was always much anti-Semitism in Austria. For this reason my father hated his Jewish name, Isidor. He felt it branded him as a Jew just as much as the yellow stars were later to brand Jews. He changed his name to Joseph, after his beloved Uncle Joseph who lived in Trieste, in Northern Italy. Joseph and his wife, Paula, had no children and they loved my father. He had lived with them after his matriculation, learning the coffee trade. He then returned to Vienna and built up the business there.

I was a happy, talkative child. When I was two years old my sister, Marta, was born. We had a governess, Ulli, and I know that she preferred my sister to me: she was quieter and better behaved! Much of my trouble in the early years of school came from the fact that I was left-handed, and I was forced to write with my right hand. My father employed

Greta and Marta with their father and Ulli outside coffee shop, Vienna, 1926.

a private teacher who came for some weeks every afternoon and I had to learn to write with my right hand and now I have quite a nice style of writing. I never learnt to cook because I was left-handed. I would go into the kitchen and my mother would say, 'Out you go!' I am sorry about that!

In 1928 my father lost much of his wealth and was forced to take on a smaller business, still in the coffee trade. He was importing coffee for a famous firm, Meindl, which is still there in Vienna. My mother used to help as well in the shop. We roasted twice a day fresh coffee. It was called Gold Kaffee and I still like that label, though of course it is not the same one.

My mother was born Frieda Rosenfeld. She was a beautiful lady who handled my father well. He was not always an easy man to live with.

I started high school in 1933, a year when anti-Semitism was growing stronger in Austria. It seemed that the people of Vienna, they learnt from babyhood what it meant to hate Jews. There is one story, of a famous public man in Vienna,

Greta with nurse, parents and chauffeur in the hills of Vienna, 1921.

a mayor, who hated the Jewish people but his best friend was a Jew! When people asked him, 'How is this?' he would say, 'I will decide who is Jewish and who is not!'

My maths teacher at school was a Nazi sympathiser: she marched under their banners on the Ringstrasse in Vienna. She hated us, the five Jewish girls. She told my father, 'Your daughter is lazy and stupid.' My father said, 'No, my daughter is very intelligent!' I am glad to say that my father took me out of this school, to another, nicer school where I did well. Then I went to business school. I knew that I wanted to work with people…maybe become a journalist. I read a lot.

When I was a little girl I learnt ballet. I like to dance very much. I also liked going to movies and reading humorous stories and I enjoyed comic acting: I think I inherited a little of my father's sense of humour! I would have liked to be an actress, but I discovered that no one wanted at this time a Jewish actress.

I had to learn French at school: it was the fashion then.

The marriage of Frieda Goldschmied's sister, Irene Rosenfeld, 1922,
Frieda and Joseph to the right of the bride. Of Frieda's family shown
here, many did not survive the war.

It would have been much better if I had learnt English. My
sister, two years later, learnt English, though she now lives
in France! Her English accent was very good: she spoke 'as
though she had a hot potato in her mouth'. We also learnt
Italian. When Uncle Joseph came from Trieste to stay, we
spoke Italian to him.

12 March 1938 was the day of the Anschluss. Our
chancellor, Kurt Schuschnigg, went to see Hitler some weeks
earlier but there was no response. The Germans invaded
Austria. We could hear the soldiers marching through
Vienna that morning, hundreds of thousands of them. The
Chancellor spoke to us on the radio: 'This is the end. I wish
everything goes well for Austria.' Of course many Austrians
were very happy to belong to the German Reich (though
they strongly denied this after the war had ended).

The summer months in Vienna in 1938 were very hard.
Jews were not allowed to go to parks or to school; they
couldn't sit on benches in the street. There was only one
public baths in Vienna for Jewish people. There I met my

Summer holiday in Austria, 1936. Figure at top left is Friedl Becker.
Greta is in front row left.

first love, Kurt Allina. He was about twenty-two and rode a motorbike. We went to the cinema together and walked on Sundays in the Vienna woods. But when my father found that I had been meeting this young man, he forbade me to see him again, and that was the end of our friendship. Later he went to Mexico.

Jews were despised in Vienna. Yet everyone liked the Goldschmieds, because my father was such a kind man. Before 1938 we used to go for summer holidays to a beautiful villa outside Vienna. Another family, the Beckers, also came every year. Then they said they would not come any more if they had to stay with Jews. But they made an exception of the Goldschmieds, because they liked us. Their son, Friedl, was two years older than me and we liked each other. He played often on the piano one of my favourite songs. In January 1938 I went to my first ball and I danced the first waltz with Friedl Becker. Then he joined the SS. He went to Russia and was killed. His parents had been very happy when the Germans came, then they lost their son.

There were so many misconceptions about Jewish people, that they were always hungry for money. But they are people like everyone else, a mixture of the good and bad. People would say to me, 'You can't be Jewish...you're so nice, like a Viennese girl!'

After the Anschluss, we were frightened: what would happen to us? Later we asked our father, 'How could we have stayed in Vienna?' knowing already what was happening in Germany. But by then, it was too late. Our friends opposite us in Vienna put a photo of Hitler in the window. We didn't dare to walk out in the streets. One man in our house jumped out of a window. A lot of people committed suicide.

Where would we go now? My mother had four sisters and four brothers. Her younger sister, Margit, lived in Vienna, the others lived in Hungary. Margit was beautiful, I always admired her. She was married to my father's cousin, Rudi, and they had a little boy, Hansi. In summer they stayed in a villa at Baden near Vienna and Margit met Paul Ehrnfeld there. She divorced Rudi and married Paul Ehrnfeld. Divorce was considered a terrible thing at the time...but I didn't realise that this new marriage would be our way of coming to Australia.

Uncle Paul bought a beautiful pensione for Margit in Vienna, where they lived after their marriage. Paul was the son of a very wealthy man, and he was a bit arrogant. Soon after the Germans arrived, on the Monday after the Saturday invasion, there was an article in the paper about his family. He was frightened, and he and his wife stayed two days with us. They brought their jewellery to us for safe-keeping. On the Wednesday, Paul and Margit returned to their pensione as it seemed safe by then.

On Thursday at two a.m. came a big knock on our door and the concierge came with six Nazis in SA uniforms. 'Where is Mr Ehrnfeld? they demanded. 'He is not here,' my father told them. 'Where is the jewellery?' they asked, and went straight to the office and found the jewellery in the office safe. One Nazi stayed behind, sitting at the table with his revolver. The others went to find Paul at the pensione.

That was the night many prominent Jews – actors, musicians, writers – were taken away. But because they had the jewellery they didn't bother taking Paul and they recalled the Nazi who was guarding the office. They left my father alone too.

Later on I found out who had betrayed the Ehrnfelds. My father's secretary for fifteen years was a secret member of the Nazi party. She worked often in father's office and had known the office safe. She also must have seen on Tuesday the Ehrnfelds staying with us. They would have taken Uncle Paul had he and Aunt Margit not left the night before. The secretary only wanted them to take the Ehrnfelds but not my father because she liked him.

The Ehrnfelds quickly got a permit to Australia, and in London they were able to retrieve a great deal of money for their jewellery from Lloyds insurance company. They came to Australia and bought a farm near Melbourne, but it was not very successful because they knew so little about the land.

Now life started to become unbearable. Jews couldn't go

to cinemas or public parks. If you walked in the street you could get abused or humiliated. You might be made to wash the floor. In restaurants, they had to crawl under the table and lick the floor…it was a shocking time.

Where could we go? It was impossible to get a visa, though Aunty Margit promised she would get us a visa to Australia. She got us one in 1939, just before the war started. By then it was too late.

My father tried to get to Hungary and from there to the States. He had two uncles in Trieste. He tried to persuade Uncle Joseph and Aunt Paula to go with him to the States. You could still leave Italy but not Austria. You couldn't take any money out of Austria, and where could we go without money? My father had never held money in Switzerland or elsewhere. In 1933 it was easier for Jews to leave Germany and there was a big exodus of writers, film producers and artists to the United States and England. But the Germans learnt how to make it more difficult.

After March 1938, we were not allowed to go to school. It was shocking to discover your friends were Nazis. No one wanted to talk to you any more. We were lucky that our father had no enemies, and we still tried to run our coffee shop. Our Ulli used to look after us while both our parents worked in the shop.

My father had a plan, to go to Trieste via Hungary. His brother-in-law was a solicitor in Budapest, who acquired Hungarian papers from the town where my father was born. (He was born in Hungary but after the first world war people had to declare themselves as citizens of Hungary or of Austria: my father had chosen Austria). At last we obtained these papers and got Hungarian passports from the Hungarian Consulate in Vienna. (I still have that passport; I only used it once.) When we received the passports, my father kissed the consul's hand: he knew that these papers would save our lives. To get them did cost a lot of money in Hungary and we couldn't send money from Vienna, so Uncle Joseph sent the money to Hungary from Trieste.

28 September 1938 is the date in the passport. My father left a week later on a train going directly to Budapest. He went alone as it would have been more dangerous for the whole family to travel together. We left some days later, on 15 October. We went to Hungary on a little train and changed to a bus which took us to a little village, Kisfalud, where my grandmother lived. We didn't take much luggage, just as though we were going on our yearly holiday to our grandmother. We got out of the bus in front of the church and walked to our grandmother's house.

Half an hour later some Hungarian gendarmes came looking for 'the two Viennese girls': they knew our identity because we visited Grandmother every year, when we had to go to the mayor, show our passport and get permission to stay. Grandmother said, 'Come back a bit later. They are asleep.' That night my Aunt Irene sent for us; we travelled by horse and carriage to her big property where no one knew us. We knew the farm, we visited there every Easter from Vienna. We thought it was so romantic to camp on the farm. They had racehorses…one was called Paprika.

We stayed two months on the farm and then caught the train to Budapest, where we were going to stay with another of my aunts, another divorced lady, married to a very wealthy man in the city. On the train we met a young man in Hungarian uniform travelling home with his father after an accident. He spoke to us in German. His name was George and he was Jewish and invited me to go on a walking excursion in the mountains near Budapest the next Sunday. My aunt didn't think that this was at all proper! However, I went with him on the excursion, with lots of other young people. I wore an Austrian dirndl, while all the Hungarian girls wore trousers! 'Who is this funny girl?' they asked themselves. Later, I overheard them ask George in a resthouse, 'Why did you bring this girl?' 'I wanted to learn German,' he said. Every young man I met in Hungary wanted to practise speaking German!

Part Two

In Budapest we had no money. My father studied at libraries and started a new job, importing cork from Spain and Portugal. He put an advertisement in the paper: 'Two sisters, born in Vienna, specialise in teaching German.' But

we only got men replying to the advertisement! My father changed the notice to 'Two sisters specialise in teaching German to children.' So we started to teach children German. We stayed with the children for an hour or for up to half a day, and their families would sometimes take us on outings, to the pool and other places. One of my students was only a few years younger than me.

Greta and Marta Goldschmied in the hills of Budapest, 1942.

My father suffered bad sinus trouble in the smoky dirty atmosphere near the railway terminus where we had an apartment. After a while we moved to a smaller apartment, but it was much nicer, just near the Danube and away from the railway station. There was one main room, a hall and a maid's room where my father slept. In Budapest, life was still very different from what it was like in Austria. People just didn't think that the Germans were only two or three hours away. We met lots of nice young people and went every Sunday in summer into the mountains. We didn't notice anti-Semitism in Hungary in 1939.

A week after we arrived in Hungary came Kristallnacht. The windows of our shop in Vienna were broken. My mother was anxious to go back to Vienna and clear up and collect what she could; but our governess, Ulli, rang us from Vienna and warned us not to come. She brought two suitcases of clothes to us in Budapest; in fact, she came twice to visit us. My father gave her written permission to stay in our apartment in Vienna.

Father got in touch with his two uncles in Trieste and tried to persuade them to come with him and the family to the United States. But they didn't want to, and they stayed in Trieste. Our family permit to Australia arrived just before war broke out, but after that there was no possibility of making use of it.

In Italy, Mussolini was no friend of Hitler but after the German army occupied Paris he joined him, which ultimately led to the downfall of the Italian Jews. One of my uncles got deported. Uncle Joseph and Aunty Paula were in hospital when they were recognised by someone who worked for the Nazis – a tailor. He reported them – 'They are the rich Goldschmieds' – and they were killed. We only found this out after the war. They should have gone to the States while they had a chance! But what do you know? People didn't want to leave their home.

Because we had come to Hungary without any money, my mother's relatives paid our rent for the first months. We were especially helped by my mother's nephew, Imre, a wealthy businessman who adored my father and loved talking politics with him. But my father wanted some independence. He became an agent for importing cork for use in wine bottles and shoes. He spoke a little Spanish and wrote to various firms and arranged to become their agent. He would walk around the city carrying a big bag...but it was very light because it was full of cork! His business prospered and soon he didn't need any more help from relatives. One good thing was that food was cheap and plentiful in Budapest, especially the fruit. I had never seen such beautiful fruit, fresh from the country. In Vienna, the fruit was always picked while it was green and hard, but here it came ripe every day to the markets. We had plenty to eat and slowly we got used to life in Hungary. We had to learn Hungarian, which was difficult at first because people wanted to talk German with us.

My father had always wanted to have a son. But when they started to call up young Jewish boys for labour camps, he was glad he had no sons. There were some anti-Semitic clauses, such as 'Numerus Clausus' in Hungary. This meant that Jews were not allowed to go to university, only the few who had connnections.

I will tell you how I came to meet my future husband, Andy Rado. He was a very intelligent man, not a businessman. He would have made a good architect, but being Jewish he was not allowed to go to university. He came to Vienna from Budapest in about 1935, in order to learn German and also learn the coffee trade. He was about twenty-one years old

Andy's passport photo.

Greta on her 20th birthday, 1941.

then. He met my father in the course of business and they struck up a friendship. In Budapest we lived near St Stephens Park. Andy also lived nearby in a beautiful apartment with his sister, overlooking the park. One Sunday afternoon he met my father there by chance while walking in the park. 'Herr Rado!' my father called out. He had a wonderful memory for names. Andy also recognised him. They started to talk business just when I arrived. I was very short-sighted and didn't like wearing glasses and did not recognise him.

Andy came to visit our home in Budapest one evening. I had just came home from teaching and there he was, a very good-looking young man in a dark coat and a white scarf, talking to my father. I rushed into the kitchen and brought out some sweets. I fell in love with him that day. I don't think he fell in love the first time like me – though he says, yes, he did!

It was 1942. Andy was called up and taken to a labour camp on the Czechoslovakian border. He used to be a lieutenant in the Hungarian army so he could still wear his army cap and had to to keep order in the labour camp. On his free days he visited his mother who lived in Miskolc not far from the camp. Sometimes he was able to come to Budapest and visit my family. After 1944 he was transferred to the border of Rumania. Andy's father had died fighting for Hungary in the First World War and so his mother had been able to save him at the last minute from being transported to Russia. He was very lucky. From this transport only two young men came back. Andy sent me once or twice a card but after that I didn't hear from him again.

In Budapest one of my uncles was president of a social club and during the war my sister and I went there and met young men who were engineers or architects.But as soon as we met them they were sent off to labour camps. Sundays we went to a Jewish club. There was music and dancing. I met a nice young man there who played the piano. He used to live in Paris. I like to sing and I liked his music. He was amazed at how good my French was! He fell in love with me. I liked him when he played the piano but I decided that he really wasn't 'my type'. I hadn't forgotten Andy…but I was a young girl. I liked company and I wanted to fall in love again! Then I met Dr Tibor Graf, a young man who had been studying in Paris and assisting Madame Curie. I met him in 1943, when he had been sent back to Hungary from Oslo where he was teaching. (The Nazis did not arrest him, because he had a Hungarian passport.) I met him at the same social club. He was a good dancer too. Our friendship grew and we went walking in the mountains near Budapest on Sundays. I didn't at this time know how very important this friendship would be to me.

19 March 1944 was a Sunday, a beautiful spring day, and my sister and I were out walking in the mountains with Tibor, my sister and two more friends. I felt so happy. I said, 'I can feel spring is coming!' People were very sober on the train going home. When we got home that day my mother said, 'The Germans have marched into Budapest.'

From then on there were curfews. We had to wear a yellow star. We were frightened about what would happen. There were rumours of deportations from the outskirts of Budapest; my father had two sisters who were deported. Tibor got in touch with me and was able to get me a Swedish

Greta's Swedish passport.

passport from the Swedish embassy where he was working. I was one of the first to get these passports: there was one for me and one for his parents, but no more. My father visited the Swedish embassy in the hills above Budapest, but there was such a long queue it was impossible to gain entry.

The hot summer months of 1944 passed. We were confined inside, just moving outside to buy a little food from time to time. My mother was a very good cook and could cook from almost nothing.

In June, Jewish people in the country outside Budapest were deported. They had the wagons ready at the station to take Jews from Budapest. But by August 1944 they decided not to deport people who were living in the inner city, as they felt this might help protect the city from Allied bombing.

On 15 October 1944, the head of the Nazi party in Hungary, Ferenc Szalasi, proclaimed that every man up to sixty was to be taken away, including my darling father. My father was a man who was not sporty or athletic; he always said, 'Jews shouldn't be sporty...they should go to the coffee house and read the paper!' Three days later, girls from fifteen up to forty also had to assemble and be taken away.

Our concierge was a Nazi. He knew I had a Swedish passport because I had told him. And when he came to take us to the assembly point he threatened me, telling me I must not take my Swedish passport with me. But I took it secretly. We were handed over to a Nazi guard and had to walk for hours and hours. In the evening we arrived at a horse-racing stadium. There were thousands of girls there and in the rain I got separated from my sister. That night I made a secret vow: 'If I survive I will never ever go to a horse race!' (I have kept that vow.)

I found my sister, and next morning we had to walk twenty kilometres or further to a disused brick factory near Veresegyhaza. The men who were working there were astonished that these young women were singing as they arrived. We had to sleep on the floor. I was so cold. It was the end of October, beginning of November and raining. I found a little hole where they burnt the bricks and my sister and I crawled in there and spent the nights there. We had had to give up our money but I kept mine hidden on me.

There were about 500 women there. In the mornings we had to march out and dig ditches against the Russian tanks. There were many poor girls, with no warm clothes or shoes. In all my life I had never seen such poor Jewish people. There was very little food, just bread you could buy from peasants. But my mother sent our cleaning woman once a week to bring us food. Some of the girls were street walkers. Five of the girls consorted with the Nazis, hoping to gain their freedom. But when the girls tried to escape, they shot them. That's when we knew, nobody can escape from here.

The guards liked to make us unhappy, playing cruel jokes. One night we all had to stand out in the cold. The guard announced, 'Those with foreign passports are to stand out!' But I thought, 'No! This is not the time.' I felt like I was back in a Shakespeare play where you are asked to step out at night. Five girls stood out; they were ordered to dig a grave. Then the guard laughed and shot his gun in the air. Then he let us all go back to the factory.

The Russians were nearing Budapest; we could hear them

nearby. Someone who wanted to help us, some high ranking Hungarian officer, came and checked which girls had Swedish, Italian or Swiss passports, but Spanish was not on their list. My mother had got us Spanish passports. I had my Swedish passport with me and I was crossed off the list with ten more girls. But the Nazi guard did not let us go without discharge papers. We had to stay there until he received the discharge papers. I hugged my sister and we both cried because she had to leave and join the many hundred girls marching towards the Austrian border. I was so terrified that this man would not let us go. I crawled in a dark hole that night and it was full of mice. The next day the papers arrived and we were marched to the train. The Nazi guard ordered us to assemble on the station when we reached Budapest, where he would be waiting for us. I was very frightened, I knew he would not let us go home. The train we caught was full of German soldiers coming back from the Russian front. A young German soldier befriended me on the train, and I told him my story and how frightened I was of the guard. When we arrived in Budapest he took my hand and took me home – a German! – much to the amazement of our caretaker. My mother invited him in and gave him some sweets and then he left. There were always some good people who tried to save us. Everyone who has been through that war has a story of at least one person who tried to help them. I never forgot that soldier, that he helped to save my life.

The next day I went to the Swedish Embassy and Tibor asked me to stay there with him. But I felt lonely. I wanted to be with my family because I knew life was going to be very difficult. Besides, much as I liked Tibor I was still in love with Andy. At that stage I didn't know whether my father was still alive. I discovered later that my father had been able to escape from the forced march towards Austria. He met up with a cousin on the march, who pushed him into a toilet where he hid from the guards, and then made his way back to Budapest. My sister had also escaped from the forced march and had returned to the city.

I left the Swedish Embassy and started walking home to our apartment. I wanted to see my parents. On the way home I saw a lovely turquoise shawl in a shop window, so I went inside to buy it because I was cold. That action saved my life. Out on the streets, the police were rounding up everyone and marching them to a brick factory on the other side of Budapest. Once I saw what was happening I didn't attempt to go home but turned round and went back to Tibor at the Embassy.

My parents too, were lucky to escape the round-up. They had been away from their apartment, going to collect my sister, Marta, who had been staying with our cleaning lady. When they returned with my sister to the empty apartment block they knew they were in danger and did not dare to stay there any longer. They took refuge in the 'Spanish House' at 38 St Stephens Park, where I joined them after receiving news of where they were. Meanwhile, Tibor had got me papers stating I was the fiancée of a Swedish employee .

There were 400 people crowded into the Spanish House. A man called Giorgio Perlasca* helped us to get the Spanish passports. He helped lots of other people too, by pretending to be the Spanish Consul and protecting us from

* Appendix One describes the work of Giorgio Perlasca in saving the lives of many Hungarian Jews.

IDENTIFICATION ET SIGNALEMENT:

de M. Izor GOLDSCHMIED
Fils de Thérèse Holstein
Age de 56 ans
Etat civil marié
Profession représentant de commerce
Taille moyenne
Visage rond
Yeux bleus
Nez droit
Bouche régulière
Cheveux etc. blonds

Izidor Goldschmied
Signature

de Mme. Izor GOLDSCHMIED
Fille de Fanny Schiller
Age de 49 ans
Etat civil mariée
Profession ménage
Taille moyenne
Visage rond
Yeux bruns
Nez droit
Bouche régulière
Cheveux etc. bruns

Goldschmied Izidorné
Signature

de Mlle. Marguerite GOLDSCHMIED
Fille de Frida Rosenfeld
Age de 23 ans
Etat civil célibataire
Profession prof. de langue
Taille moyenne
Visage rond
Yeux bleus
Nez droit
Bouche régulière
Cheveux etc. bruns

Margit Goldschmied
Signature

de Mlle. Marthe GOLDSCHMIED
Fille de Frida Rosenfeld
Age de 21 ans
Etat civil célibataire
Profession prof. de langue
Taille moyenne
Visage rond
Yeux bleus
Nez droit
Bouche régulière
Cheveux etc. blonds

Martha Goldschmied
Signature

Nº 67

PASSEPORT-COLLECTIF
PROVISOIRE

Nous, Consul d'Espagne à Budapest

faisons savoir à tous ceux qui verront le présent passeport espagnol que: Monsieur et Madame Izidor Goldschmied, et leurs filles Marguerite et Marthe

partent de cette ville à destination de: Madrid

Prions en conséquence toutes les autorités civiles et militaires, auxquelles ce passeport sera présenté, de laisser librement passer les porteurs et de leur donner, en cas de besoin, tout aide et protection pour leur voyage.

Le présent passeport est valable jusque au 10 Janvier 1945 pour se rendre en territoire espagnol

Consulat d'Espagne à Budapest.

le 10 Octobre 1944.

Le Consul:

Este pasaporte no podrá ser renovado sin un permiso especial del Ministerio de Asuntos Exteriores de Madrid.

The family's Spanish passport, which saved their lives during the war.

the Germans. We got a room for the four of us on the 6th floor of the building. The house was on the end of the park and close to the Danube. We felt safer there, with all these people seeking sanctuary with the Spanish Consul. From the windows we could see in the park below where people were standing in lines, waiting to be deported.

The concierge looked after us. When the police called he rang Perlasca, who told the police that we were all Spanish. Giogio Perlasca was in fact a friend of my father. They had met often through my father's import business from Spain and my father had known that Perlasca really was an Italian. Once when the police came, we had to make a quick escape, because the concierge could not get in touch with Perlasca. We climbed

from the sixth floor out onto the balcony and then to the sixth floor of a neighbouring building. We hid in a big case where all the summer furniture was stored. I made another vow to my sister and mother while we were in hiding. If I survived I would never cry at the pictures…but do you know I still do cry at the pictures.

The Spanish house, 38 St Istvan Park, Budapest.
The 6th floor where the family lived from November 1944
until the end of January 1945 is clearly visible.

Part Three

From our hiding place we listened and finally heard my father call out, 'You can come back, the police have gone.'

A very difficult period began. We couldn't go down to the cellar, we left that for the old people, who were more frightened about their lives than the young people. The bombing was very heavy. I knew that the bombs would fall on everyone, whether you are a Jew or not.

The Russians were very near by now. I would go to collect water from the Danube and people would ask, seeing me come out of the Spanish House, 'Are you Spanish?' I used to say, 'Yes, sort of.'

The Russians arrived, one by one. We were very happy; we thought our troubles were over now. What does the word 'Jew' mean in Russian? I learnt this Russian word: 'Jewrey'. I wanted to tell them that we were not German but Jewish. I told a Russian soldier, 'I am a Jew', and he hit me. He was from the Ukraine, where they were just as anti-Semitic as the Germans.

The Russians built a wooden bridge across the Danube; all the older bridges had been bombed. One evening we left the Spanish House and went out into the city, looking for food. We could hear gunshots quite close, between Russians and Germans. Budapest is actually made up of two cities: Buda and Pest. The Germans had already left Pest and on 15 January 1945 Buda also was freed from the Germans.

On that first evening we walked to my cousin's factory where we found friends. My father found a chair and sat on it and the three of us – Mother, my sister and I – sat on his knee and we all cried bitterly. We felt that we had been saved.

After the Germans left we went back to find our apartment at Legrady Karoly-utca 48b but it was empty. We had been living at Legrady Karoly-utca since 1939. In the winter of 1944 the apartment block came under the protection of Raoul Wallenberg* and the Swedish embassy and was declared a safe house for Jews. It was one of a number of 'Swedish Houses' where Jews could seek refuge if they had a Swedish passport. The caretaker had been told that as the house was under the protection of the Swedish embassy it was untouchable by the Nazis. But we had to leave because only I had a Swedish passport and the rest of my family didn't.

We found out later that our absence from the house during December had actually saved our lives. On 30 and again on 31 December 1944, the caretaker's Nazi friends from Obuda, on the outskirts of Budapest, arrived to empty all apartments for the SS to use. All the Jewish people in the house were taken out, marched over to the Danube and shot. We were in the Spanish House at that time, and we did not dare to look out the windows down into the park where so many people were being killed. Sometimes it is very very strange the way things happen. That could have been us, if we had been still living at our former apartment. From all the Jewish

* The story of Raoul Wallenberg and his heroic rescue of many Hungarian Jews is described in Appendix Two.

people in that apartment block, only two survived. We were the lucky ones, for both parents and two girls to survive.

We came back to our apartment and found it empty, but we were frightened of the caretaker, we didn't trust him. What if the Germans came back? So we went to another apartment, one that belonged to one of my aunts who had been deported. We slept on the floor with another couple for some days. The front door had been broken down and one night two Russian soldiers came in and grabbed my mother and my sister. I rushed out onto the balcony in my bare feet. Anything was better than to be grabbed by these men. My father screamed, like an animal who sees its children taken away. The soldiers became confused and dropped their lamp and then ran away. I had a fit of crying, 'We are saved, we are not saved...' Life was so uncertain.

After this, Father took us to another place, a big apartment where there were about twenty other people. The caretaker spoke Russian and he protected us. When Russian soldiers came for women he said, 'They are all old and sick.' The soldiers were very afraid of sickness so then they would leave us alone.

We had to walk for hours to the markets to buy food. People didn't like to take money, it was worth so little. My father was like a skeleton, because everything he got he gave to us.

Once we finally returned to our apartment in mid-January, we had to repair it, clean the windows, fix broken doors, obtain food. No one wanted money. We gave jewellery, whatever we had, to obtain food. 8 February was my birthday. I dreamt of eating potatoes.

Nearly every day I walked to the house where Andy used to live, but there was no news. I got a letter from Tibor. My sister and I walked through the snow for nearly an hour to the apartment where he lived with his parents. They were all safe and we promised to see more of each other. When we walked home we saw a light in the kitchen. Who was there sitting at the table with my parents? Andy! I was so happy. He believed that his mother, plus his sister and her little boy, had been killed at Auschwitz.

From then on we met often; he was living with his other sister and his brother-in-law. Andy was helping his brother-in-law, who had a mechanical business and a shop. At lunch time the shop was empty, and there Andy asked me for the first time for my hand. It was not very romantic: he said, 'Greta, do you think I can keep you?' He meant in the style I had been used to! And then we kissed. We were both very happy.

There was no engagement party. Father felt it was not a good time to get married but we still met very often. Andy got a job and I was working too. My father decided to go back to Vienna to try and sort out his business there. My sister, Marta, was keen to leave Hungary so she went back with him on the train to Vienna. The journey on the train, full of Russian soldiers, took nearly all day. At one stage my father and sister were made to leave the train, but a high-ranking Russian officer approached them and helped them to get back on. His name was Mischa. He sat with them on the train and explained that he too was Jewish and his parents had been killed in the war. 'I'm a journalist,' he said, 'and I travel from Budapest to Vienna each week. You can come with me back to Budapest when you wish.'

When they reached Vienna, my father and sister walked to our apartment in the Russian zone. Then my father left to go to the US zone where my mother's sister was again living. Marta went up to our apartment and our governess opened the door: 'This is unbelievable!' she said. 'I cried so much for you! I thought all the Jews had been killed!'

Marta was given a small room in the apartment. Ulli had rented out all the other rooms, and she had sold lots of our beautiful silverware and paintings. That was how she managed to live.

After spending some time in Vienna in the US zone, Father decided it was still too early to think of returning to Vienna. There was very little food, while in Budapest at least we now had enough to eat. But Marta decided that she would stay in Vienna. She spoke very good English and was able to get a job with the British Red Cross. Father returned to Budapest on the train with Mischa. Eventually he decided that we would all return to Vienna. First I had to go and then he would follow after he finished his business in Budapest. He arranged with Mischa that I would travel to Vienna on the train with him. Andy would follow later on. There was really no future for us now in Hungary.

On that trip I was the only woman on the train! But then another woman came on board, who was looking for her husband who'd been in a labour camp. When we arrived in Vienna, at night, Mischa took both of us to our apartment, because the woman had nowhere to stay. Our governess got such a shock when she opened the door and saw me with another woman and a Russian soldier! She gave me a small room in the apartment, where my father used to have his office, and I stayed there. Marta was there too, working with the Red Cross during the day and going out at night to the British zone. We went dancing there. That was something quite new to me: in Budapest we were not used to going out to dancing yet. I met some very nice soldiers, who were so charming in their US uniforms. But I cried after Andy; I missed him.

After two weeks in Vienna I went back to the station looking for Mischa. I pleaded with him to take me home. He was very upset. 'I can't take you. Your father won't like that!' But at last he agreed to take me.

When we arrived in Budapest I walked home and my parents opened the door. 'Are you crazy, to come back?' they cried. Then the door bell rang and there was Andy, he was coming to ask how I was. From then on I knew I would not leave him. Andy had got a job through a friend, managing the PX store at the US Embassy. It was a very good job, he had the use of a jeep and a driver and he was paid in US dollars. He was very intelligent and he knew where to get the food supplies for the stores.

Andy Rado with the two sisters.

New Year's Eve

37

1945 came. We knew that we would have to get married the next year. My parents decided to go back to Vienna. Father went first and Mother was to go later, after our wedding. On 8 June 1946, we were married at a registry office. My mother was there, a cousin and Andy's sister. There was no wedding breakfast. We went straight to the train and had two days' honeymoon at a small pensione on Lake Balaton. I made the booking – I used to go there as a young girl. The weather was beautiful and we were very happy. We had to pay for everything in gold. Every day, money was worth less and less.

Back in Budapest we had our own apartment. Soon I discovered that I was pregnant. To have the baby in Vienna would have been very difficult, so we decided to stay in Budapest.

Greta and Andy Rado with Susi, Budapest, 1947.

On 6 February 1947, darling little Suzie arrived, seven weeks premature. She was only about two kilograms twenty but she grew up very beautifully. Andy left the US Embassy job and got a job with a big coffee firm. All the businesses were now run by the state.

We wanted to emigrate to Australia, but as time went on it became very difficult to leave Hungary – nearly impossible. We had a permit for three people, but we were refused a passport. Susi was already eighteen months old and again we were refused a passport.

We decided to escape...but how? My father lost four of his sisters at Auschwitz but his younger brother survived and was living in the country on my grandparents' farm. I rang him and asked to come and visit him. You couldn't talk about your real plans on the phone. But he was an intelligent man and he would have guessed why I was coming.

One Sunday I left Budapest on the train. After two hours I changed trains and arrived at the town of Kapuvar where my uncle met me. He took me home to Kisfalud. I told him of our plans and he said he would try to help us. He had a friend in Kapuvar who he thought would be able to help us.

In Budapest the situation was so dangerous we decided to leave as soon as possible. We were to ring my uncle and tell him 'We are coming for the big wedding celebration.'

We only told Andy's sister and we gave her our cash but we left everything else behind. Our little maid knew nothing about it. We took a rucksack and a little potty for Susi – she had been trained to use the potty since she was a year old. We travelled by train to Kapuvar and our uncle's friend met us there. That night one of the smugglers who

Susi in her lambswool babysack.

had been hired drove us to Lake Neusiedler See between Hungary and Austria. We hoped Susi wouldn't cry. Once the police stopped us and we said we were going to a funeral in Sopron near the Austrian border. We stayed at a small village that night and they hid us in a stable, it was terrible, so very cold.

In the morning a car pulled by a horse took us to the lake. Two other smugglers arrived in a little boat. We stepped into the boat. Susi was warmly dressed in a babysack lined with lambswool, only her head visible, all wrapped up. The lake was very shallow at first and the two men navigated with large poles like in Venice. Then it became very windy. The water blew into the boat and we had to help the men bail it out. It was so icy cold…it was late November and already snowing in Austria.

After six hours we came to an island on the Austrian border where two other smugglers were supposed to meet us. They didn't arrive and the other men did not want to wait. 'We will leave you here and the others will soon come.' 'But what will I do with the little girl?' I cried. 'She will die here in the cold.' I gave them my beautiful watch and they agreed to take us further in the boat, to the Austrian side of the border. Altogether we were seven hours in that little boat.

When we reached the border we had to jump out of the boat as the two men were anxious to get back to Hungary. Andy nearly fell out of the boat, carrying Susi in her sack.

Neusiedler See, scene of the Rados' escape (route marked) from Hungary to Moerbisch in Austria.

There was a bus we were to catch at three p.m., but luckily we missed it! The authorities would have checked everyone's papers and sent us back because we had none. We had thrown all our Hungarian papers into the lake.

At the border we walked to a little hut where some Gypsies were staying. 'From where are you coming?' they asked. 'From the lake? In this weather?' I pleaded with them to lend me a little money so I could ring my father in Vienna. A little gypsy girl walked with me to the post office and I rang my father. He warned me to be very careful, to watch whom I spoke to as there were many police around.

A man heard my Viennese accent, a Mr Koenig. He looked curiously at me. 'Who can she be, speaking Viennese so beautifully in this little country town?' he thought. 'Where are you from?' he asked. It turned out that he knew my mother's relatives, the Rosenfelds, who had been living close by. He was in the wine business. 'How can I help you?' he asked. I said I wanted to go to Vienna. He promised to help us get a cab to Vienna, and told us to come back when it was dark.

I then had to try to find my way back to where Susi and Andy were hiding. I knew the hut was near a field where boys were playing soccer, so I asked some people, 'Can you tell me where they play soccer? My nephew plays there.' So they directed me back to the gypsy hut. When I got back there I found Susi was quite happy, playing with the gypsy children.

We met Mr Koenig when it got dark, and he warned us not to speak Hungarian. A taxi came for us and Mr Koenig gave us 400 schillings. How should we pay him back? He said, 'I go every day for coffee to the Kaffee Landman next to the Burgtheater in Vienna.' That's where we agreed to meet him.

The taxi man was very nice; he went a back way through the woods and fields to Vienna and finally I met my father at the pensione, late at night. My parents couldn't believe that we had made it there. The apartment was full of people: my parents, my aunt, and other relatives staying there.

Next day my father went with me to the Kaffee Landman; we paid Mr Koenig and thanked him very much for what he had done.

The following day Andy and I went to a police station in the US zone, where we were fined fifty schillings each for having crossed the border without permits or passports: very strange, because I was born in Vienna! I still have the receipts for paying those fines.

I was so happy to be back in Vienna. But as Winston Churchill said, the Iron Curtain was falling. It was dangerous to move out of the British or US zones into the Russian zone as they always asked for documents and we had none. We heard of so many Hungarians being caught without papers and being sent back to Hungary.

I was keen to stay in my beloved Vienna but Andy wanted to emigrate. My father said, 'Why doesn't Andy go first, and you follow later?' But no, he needed me. We wanted to stay together.

We went to the British Embassy to ask for our papers, as we had nothing with us.

Part Four

January 1949. It was snowing in Vienna and we went sledding with Susi in the Vienna Woods. It was a very happy time for me; we had a nice room in the pensione and we were with my parents. We enjoyed my mother's cooking!

Soon we had company; my mother's oldest sister and family escaped from Hungary and joined us in Vienna. Other people joined us from Hungary as well. One family had a little girl, so Susi had a friend to play with.

My parents were very sad, though, because our papers had at last arrived and it was just a question of time before we left for Australia. We heard that my mother's youngest sister, who had migrated to Melbourne, had cancer and was returning to Vienna. That meant we would not have any family to stay with in Australia. Father tried to persuade us to stay in Austria. We could perhaps have stayed in Salzburg which was in the US zone, but not in Vienna.

We had a little party on 6 February 1949. Susi was two years old and I was twenty-eight on 8 February. Susi was a beautiful little girl. She started to speak German already.

In April we started to pack and prepare for our long journey to Australia. It was so sad; we did not know whether we would ever see our family again. We might never come back to Europe: the Cold War was on and maybe there would be another war. One didn't know. Letters sent from Vienna were censored, so later on my father had to give letters to his friends for them to post from Tirol or Salzburg. And telephone calls were very expensive. You had to wait for half an hour or longer to get a connection.

Susi and Andy with the Goldschmieds. The last goodbye before leaving Vienna, 1949.

Our biggest problem now was how we were going to leave Vienna. You needed special permission. My father went to the British Consulate and bought us tickets on one of British European Airways' little planes. From the British European Airways office a car marked 'British' took us to Vienna airport. We were lucky that we weren't stopped. The plane was very small, only taking about ten passengers. It was my first flight but I wasn't frightened. I was relieved to be leaving Austria, not to be leaving my parents, but because my husband was always in danger of being taken back to Hungary.

The plane landed in Venice. It was beautiful there. It was two days before Easter and we had two hours to spare before we caught the train to Genoa. We went to the Piazza San Marco, where my parents had a photo taken on their honeymoon. I am very sentimental and I wanted to have a photo taken there too. 'Oh! You want to spend money already!' Andy exclaimed. 'No, I like to have the photo…such a precious photo for me,' I said. Susi started chasing after the pigeons and then we sat down and had a little lunch before going to the station.

Venice, 1949, en route to Australia.

At Genoa, people we knew from Budapest got us accommodation in a little hotel, just outside of the city where it was cheaper. The Italian owners of the little hotel had a little boy but had always wanted a girl, so they loved Susi. She was always smiling and talking.

We stayed in Genoa for about ten days while we waited for the ship. We admired the town: how nicely and fashionably everyone was dressed! After the war that was a new thing for us. My father gave me a gold coin and I exchanged it for a very nice pink knitted jacket – I wore it for years and years in Australia. I fell in love with Italy. One day I hoped to come back there. I spoke very fluent Italian because my father wanted to please his two uncles in Trieste.

My father had helped us organise the trip to Australia. He paid for a small cabin on the ship, *Ugolino Vivaldi*; he was able to do this through his Trieste connections. It was a converted troop ship but we found out that it wasn't in very

Andy, Greta and Susi at a hotel near Genoa, 1949

Greta and Susi, Venice, 1949.   good shape, it had just been put on to carry passengers from Europe to Australia. We got quite a shock when we went on board…we found out that our cabin had been sold to someone else! We never got a refund for this.

The ship was very primitive, with no stabiliser or air conditioning. Andy slept in a cabin with nine other men and Susi and I slept with nine other women. There was very little space. On the deck we sat next to the kitchen hands peeling potatoes. It was not very comfortable but Susi loved it …she called it 'Susi's ship'. To have our meals we climbed down a big ladder and sat at long wooden tables with some Italian people. So Susi started learning Italian. Most of the people on the ship were Italian; they sang their favourite Italian songs, all wondering whether they would ever come back to Europe.

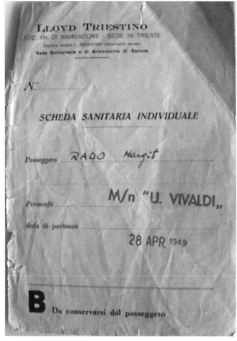

Greta's ticket on the Ugolino Vivaldi, 1949.

In Budapest we had had a very nice lady doctor who had advised us to train Susi from one year old to use a potty. She said that would make life much easier for us. When we fled Hungary we took the potty with us. On the ship she would sit on the potty and I would look around the room. 'Where is she now,' I wondered. With the rolling of the ship she had slid across the room!

Susi was always smiling and happy; everyone liked her, including the big chef. But he died when the ship called at Ceylon and after that we didn't have a chef any more.

It seemed a very long trip but eventually we arrived in Melbourne – from a European summer to an Australian winter. It was 5° in the morning…we froze! Aunty Margit was back in Vienna by then and her son met us at the wharf. Hansi and his wife Ruth were from the Dandenongs and didn't know Melbourne, so they couldn't really help us. We stayed in a little guest house on St Kilda Road, called 'Aloha'. But it was far from being Hawaiian! I started to clean rooms in the morning to help us pay the rent but it was impossible;

461 St Kilda Road, Melbourne.

Susi had to stay in bed till lunch time. Luckily Andy found a job with Holden, so we were able to move to a different guest house, at 461 St Kilda Road. It was much nicer, and provided breakfast and dinner. I could go for a walk with Susi in Faulkner Park behind the guest house. I was looking for a kindergarten which Susi could attend.

Andy met other Hungarians at the factory: there were doctors, lawyers, all types. He earned £8 a week. We paid nearly all of that for our guest house. There was no building going on in Melbourne during the war and accommodation was very expensive.

My father wrote to me about a distant cousin who lived in Melbourne and we tried to get in touch with her. We were told that she didn't live any more but her husband invited us round to dinner on Friday night. They were very upset that Andy had no hat. Andy didn't own a hat! They were so religious…they never invited us again.

Later on I asked this man about accommodation. There was a polio epidemic and we wanted to move from the

49

guesthouse. His daughter was asking £350 key money for her flat. I wrote to my father and he immediately sent us the money. One evening I went to inspect the house in Havelock Street, a little street in St Kilda. It looked very nice, all the lamps were on. However, when we moved in we found it was very dark, with not enough windows. A man at the nearby delicatessen told us the flat had been on the market for a long time and they had charged us a very high price for it, £100 more than the advertised price. These 'religious' people took every single thing from the house before we moved in, including the curtain rods and bathroom fittings. But I was happy just to have a place where I could cook for Susi and we could catch a tram into the city and into the other suburbs, which suited Andy as we couldn't afford a car. The house was very near Luna Park and we went to the beach when it was warm.

Melbourne was sometimes very hot and then overnight there would be a storm and it would turn very cold. Susi began going two days a week to Kindergarten and on the other days I looked after children at our place and they all played together. I bought Susi a doll's pram for her third birthday.

Andy met some nice people – mainly Hungarians – at work and at weekends we went out together, walking. One very nice couple had a car and we went around with them, and to the cinema. We lived near two cinemas so we would buy tickets for Saturday night. Our neighbours were very nice; they had no children and they loved Susi. On the Saturday night they looked after her. I was looking for a job but it was very hard to find a part-time job. I was happy to be in a free country but I missed my parents and I knew no Viennese people, though there were many in Melbourne. My dream was to move to Sydney.

After the war, my father had news from a solicitor in Trieste. He found out that both his uncles had been killed. Their will stated that he would inherit their business and their properties. The business firm didn't exist any more, a lot of things had been stolen from it during the war. But there was a house and an apartment he would inherit. Father persuaded my mother to move to Trieste to this beautiful apartment and he would start a business there. But my mother didn't speak Italian and didn't like it there so my father sold both properties and they returned to Vienna.

Greta's parents on their trip to Australia, 1951.

In 1951 my parents decided to join us in Australia: the Korean War was on and they were frightened that another world war was going to start. I got the permits for them. They booked first-class tickets on the *Stratheden* and came to Melbourne. My father had been importing coffee for big firms in Austria and he hoped he would be able to do the same thing over here. My father was a diligent man and straight away he tried to get connections here. But he found that 'Australians don't drink coffee!' It would take years for them to change. Now of course, in 2007, there are cafés on every street corner. And we have an opera house too! Also in 1950, people from Europe complained, 'You can't get this vegetable, you can't get that...' A lot of the Italians who came out started to plant vegetables and fruit and now you can buy everything in Australia, much more than in Vienna.

In Melbourne my parents stayed at 461 St Kilda Road. There they met a very nice Dutch couple; he was a textiles importer. They invited Andy to come and work for them and he was very happy to do so.

My father liked to drink a glass of wine and enjoy the company of friends. In Vienna he loved to go with my mother to the wine places where people sat at long tables singing and laughing. In Melbourne he said to me, 'Come out and we will have a nice glass of wine together.' He was astonished to find that there were no women allowed in the hotel! He came outside, it was a quarter to six and he said, 'They order four glasses of beer at once and drink them one after another... they just stand there and don't talk to each other!' If we went to a restaurant, we had to order the wine that morning.

'This is not a country for us,' my father said. 'First, I can't import coffee here. And I can't even have a little social life over a glass of wine!' So my parents decided to go back to Vienna. The Korean War was over now and life seemed safer. My mother and father only stayed six weeks in Australia. They returned on the *Orcades*, first class again.

My heart was breaking…to leave me here with that little girl. Later on I understood that it would have been very difficult for them. Another English couple they met coming out six weeks ago on the same ship and became friends with, were on board, also going back home. They kissed my parents, and both couples were happy to see each other again. But my parents cried and I cried bitterly. The French say, 'Partir c'est un peu mourir.'

Before they left, we visited Sydney to see my mother's sister in Cremorne, who had a little business in North Sydney. A year later their son went to Melbourne, where there were already Italians setting up espresso machines. When he came back they set up the first espresso machines and gelateria in Sydney.

After visiting Sydney we flew back to Melbourne, where Andy met us at the airport. Where we had stayed in Sydney, in every house on the street there were Hungarians. Susi started to observe them as they walked along the street speaking loudly in Hungarian. On the bus from the airport, Susie told Andy, 'Daddy, there are some English-speaking people in Sydney too.' A person on the bus commented, 'We hope so!'

After my parents left on the ship, I cried a lot and felt so lonely again. I would do anything to move to Sydney. I feel the cold very much and Sydney's climate was better for me. I hoped one day we will be able to live in Sydney.

It was 1952. Andy had a good job in the Dutch firm. They liked us and invited us to parties. I could sing all the old Viennese songs. Susi was nearly five and started school in January. She liked going to school. 'We put your daughter in the Methodist class for religion,' her teachers told me.

But Susi said, 'I'm not a Methodist.' Her teachers asked her, 'What are you?' 'I don't know, I think I'm a little bit Jewish,' Susi replied.

I saw an advertisement from a woman in Sydney who wanted to exchange flats and move to Melbourne. She visited us and fell in love with our fancy room heater. I had paid £30 for it when Andy was only earning £8 a week. We were in luck: she was happy to exchange flats but said we must leave her the heater. Her place was in Cremorne, very near our relations. She told me to inspect the flat but I must go there before ten o'clock in the morning. My cousin took me to the flat, opposite Primrose Park. It was a very nice apartment, three big rooms and a bathroom and kitchen. The landlady was happy; she had a little girl like Susi. After we arrived we found that she was an alcoholic, completely drunk after ten in the morning. We were nice to her and hoped for the best.

We stayed there six years but they were not always easy. Susi went to the local public school at Neutral Bay and liked it very much. She stayed with our neighbour, Elsa, after school. I worked in a children's wear shop. My boss spoke Hungarian and German but he was very rude and I gave it up after three months. Nobody else had stayed longer than a week with him!

In Martin Place I met a friend of Andy's from Budapest, who told me about a foreign bookshop whose owner was from Vienna. 'I really need someone who speaks Hungarian,' the owner told me. 'I speak Hungarian,' I said. She didn't believe me at first but her Hungarian employee confirmed that indeed I did.

I liked that job. I like books and the customers were very

interesting. I could speak Hungarian, German, Italian and English in the shop. I had already worked in a bookshop in Melbourne and there I learnt a lot about the business. But the bookshop owner was not very nice – she didn't like people exchanging books. I worked till four o'clock and on Saturday mornings. One morning Susi was sick and I rang in saying that I would be late. 'You be in at nine o'clock or you're fired,' she said. When I came in at ten o'clock, instead of paying me two weeks' notice because I had worked for nine months, she said, 'You have to work two more weeks, then you're out!' In those two weeks, I told all the customers, 'I won't be here any more.'

I decided I would start my own little bookshop. One customer's former husband, a German, imported magazines. I sold them on commission, which was very difficult. One day I went up to a shop at 173 Pitt Street, next to the GPO. It was rented by a Lithuanian tailor and I was trying to sell him a subscription. Andy said, 'Ask him if you can rent a corner of his room.' He had no room, but there was another room close by, used by a nice old couple who sat in deckchairs – they were real estate agents but they only came in for a few hours a week. They let me have the front of the room.

That's how my business started. Andy helped me set up. He had been transferred to the same job in Sydney and he helped me on Saturdays and in his lunch hour. We put up shelves and I bought German books from importers and second-hand Hungarian books. My father helped me again, he bought new Hungarian books from the Yugoslav city of Novisd on the Danube and then I sold them. We were the only ones with new Hungarian books in Sydney.

Greta in her Pitt Street shop.

There was a nice atmosphere in my little bookshop. People liked to come in and have a little chat and tell me their problems.

In 1956 came the Hungarian uprising. Many thousands of Hungarians came to Sydney and many wanted to buy dictionaries to learn English. My father helped me import new dictionaries from Vienna. We became very well known and that's when I really learnt to speak Hungarian. Susi also learnt Hungarian and she was able to help her teacher understand the words of some of the children in her class.

My parents wanted us to come and visit them and they sent money for air tickets. Andy took a month's holiday and stayed to mind the shop. Air tickets were very expensive then. Over twenty people came to the airport to farewell us! It was the first time I had left Andy but my parents were so good to me that I had to do that. Also I would be able to have a look at things for my business.

Part Five

This was 1957. After only eight years in Australia, we were able to go back to visit Europe. I had mixed feelings about the trip: I was happy to be going to see my parents but very sad that Andy couldn't come too. We chose to travel in a Pan American clipper *Flying Cloud*. We left Sydney on 30 June 1957. We had chosen Pan American because they flew directly to Vienna from New York.

Our first stop was Fiji, which was hot and humid and we were tired after the flight in the small plane. Then to Canton Island for refuelling and on to Hawaii. In the hotel in Honolulu I was astonished at breakfast to see a string hanging out of the teapot! It was one of the new teabags. We enjoyed the beach and went for dinner enjoying the Hawaiian dancers.

After Honolulu, we had two days of sightseeing in Los Angeles. The taxis travelled so fast! We were not used to that. Then we left for New York. My first impression of this city was how rude the taxi drivers were. In Australia in the 1950s the taxi drivers were always nice and friendly and polite. We were taken to our hotel opposite Central Park. We went for afternoon tea at a little coffee shop...it was so expensive! It belonged to the big Plaza Hotel. When I arrive in a new city I always look for bookshops and in New York I bought lots of books. I had a shock when we were leaving because of the excess weight I had to pay for.

In Vienna we were very excited to see my parents. There were kisses and hugs – they looked at how big Susi had grown! They took us to their beautiful new apartment. It was on the top floor of a block in the third district, where many elegant old houses had been restored. It was near the Botanic Gardens and you could also see the Belvedere Palace. My father told me that on 15 May 1955 that was the place where Dulles, Pinay, Macmillan and Molotov, the foreign ministers of the US, France, England and Russia, had signed a treaty for the independence and neutrality of Austria. That had happened just two years ago. My parents were so relieved that there would be no more war.

My mother, a fabulous cook, spoiled us and Susi was very happy. I showed Susi our old apartment block in the fourth district. We went up there but nobody was home. I showed her where my old school was, where I used to go skating…I showed her the Opera House, everything. My parents took us to Schonbrunn to visit the beautiful castle. Then in the Prater I went with Susi on the big ferris wheel. My parents said, 'We have to go up the mountains to Semmering.' There was once a beautiful hotel, the Panhans, but it was destroyed during the occupation and was not yet restored. So we stayed five days in another hotel, the Sudbahn Hotel. Susi enjoyed the mountains and the beautiful views and mountain air. But my father could not take the high altitude so my parents returned to Vienna. Susi and I went up a mountain called Hirschen Kogel in a chairlift, sitting one behind the other. We were so frightened that we decided that we had better walk down…but it was a very long walk!

Susi made some friends at the hotel and later she met them

again in Vienna. She tried already to talk a little German with my parents. My father said, 'You better always speak German because if they hear you speaking English, prices will go up everywhere.'

My father knew a very good eye specialist and we took Susi to see if she needed glasses. 'I have to speak German!' she whispered to me when we got there. She told the specialist, 'I really can't speak or read German because I come from Australia…and we haven't got much money.' It was so sweet, we laughed about that. For me it was easy being in Austria, I have never forgotten my Viennese dialect; even now I can speak it well.

Then it was time for farewells and we both cried on the plane to Paris. My sister took us to her apartment – it was so hot! Paris in the summer heat is not very comfortable. We couldn't sleep much at night, but during the day we walked everywhere – along the Seine, to the Arc de Triomphe, the Eiffel Tower… We ate such fabulous food at the little bistros. Then off to London, where I took Susi's photo with the guards at Buckingham Palace.

Again on the plane, this time to San Francisco. Susi told the taxi driver, 'We have got a much nicer bridge in Sydney!'

On the plane back home we met two nice young girls, the famous swimmers Dawn Fraser and Laraine Crabb. The plane had to stay in Fiji but we managed to get seats on a Qantas flight to Sydney.

Andy was so happy to see us! When she was back at school at Neutral Bay Primary School, Susi had to tell the students all about the trip.

I went back to my little shop in Pitt Street, on the second floor next to the General Post Office. It was 1957; so many Hungarians were coming to Australia. There was as yet no Hungarian Consulate in Sydney, so they came to my little shop with all their problems. I was very busy; if I had to take some mail, I put up a little sign on the door, 'Back in five minutes'. Andy decided that he would have to leave his job and help me in the shop. As well, we sometimes employed part-time help.

Among those who came to the shop were many young Hungarian men who didn't speak English and were lonely and homesick. We were the only place they could go to for advice. They would come to me and ask me to book a passage to return home. I decided to become a travel agent, so that I would be able to find out the best and cheapest way for them to travel to Hungary. I would put them in touch with the Hungarian Embassy in London, which would provide papers for them to return home. But the official documents they were sent only provided them with a one-way passage to Hungary. Such travellers also needed Italian and Austrian transit visas. But it wasn't an easy job to get these: the consulates weren't too keen to give even a transit visa to people with only one paper to go back to Hungary. I had to plead very often with these officials for them to release the paperwork.

In 1958 we started to have trouble with our landlady. The rents were pegged so they could not be raised but a new law stated that one might put up the rent when a new tenant arrived. Our landlady was determined to get rid of us. She threatened, 'I will torment you until you leave!' After she and her friends broke into our apartment one night, the police had to come out, so we decided it was time to leave and find our own home. The first place we looked at was a little too expensive but the following week, after responding to a newspaper advertisement, we met an agent who drove us down to have a look at a house in a street that we knew. The setting was spectacular, with a beautiful view of the harbour. Andy came and liked it too. We really didn't want to buy such an expensive house but we had to get out of our apartment. My father helped us with the deposit.

When we were still in our flat in Cremorne, Susi came running up to me one Saturday just before Christmas 1955. 'Mummy, come quickly. There are a lot of Hungarians running round in the park!' It turned out that they were members of the Hungarian athletic team training for the 1956 Olympics. When I went down to meet them, their host invited us to a cocktail party and later also a New Year's Eve party to meet the team. The party, held on New Year's Eve of 1955, was held in a house just opposite the one we were eventually to buy. Members of the team asked me, 'In what sport is your husband?' I told them, 'My husband enjoys sports and likes reading about sport.'

On 8 October 1958 we moved into our dream house. Now it is 8 October 2007…we moved there forty-nine years ago.

Susi finished her last year as the top student at Neutral Bay Primary School, so it was easy for me to put her in to North Sydney Girls High School. There she met very nice, clever girls and became good friends with them. She liked North Sydney. As she had developed a talent for languages, she studied French, German and Latin. We were very proud and excited when the results for the Leaving Certificate for 1964 were published in the papers and Susan Rado gained a maximum pass with first-class honours in Latin, French and German and As in English and Maths.

By this time we were very well-known as a travel agency and I became an agent for two big shipping companies. Hungarians who were already naturalised Australians would come in to see us and arrange for passports and ask for visas to visit Hungary. Again my father helped. He befriended the official Hungarian travel agency in Vienna and had the passports stamped there, and then sent them back to me. Other travel agents couldn't understand how I managed to get my clients their Hungarian visas!

At that time, people were becoming interested in buying handicrafts. I remembered the beautiful handiwork I had seen in Hungary and my father supported my idea that I should try importing some fabrics and handicrafts to sell in Australia.

In 1960 I lost my mother but I was unable to go over to Europe then. In 1964 we thought it would be good for me to go and visit my father in Vienna. While over there I planned to visit Hungary to enquire about importing goods to Australia. You could only import from one firm that was owned by the state.

From Vienna I caught the train to Budapest. I had mixed feelings about going back to Budapest. I was warned in Vienna, 'Do not speak Hungarian!' On the train everyone sat silently. In the compartment I had a window seat and I was astonished that nobody spoke. The passport officials came round. The Austrian officials were quite nice but the Hungarians were very severe. They looked at me and at my passport: 'Born in Vienna'. They asked me in Hungarian if I had anything to declare but I pretended that I didn't understand. It was difficult for me; I am naturally a talkative person.

At the station in Budapest I was met by a young lady, Eva, from the state-owned export company. It was called Modex and later Hungarocorp. Eva was good-looking and smartly dressed, and spoke perfect German. She accompanied me to my hotel. Next day she introduced me to her boss and they showed me some samples of the work. They decided that we should go for a trip to the countryside and see the handicrafts actually being made. We travelled out to a beautiful little village called Mezokovesd and saw the women making hand-embroidered blouses, children's wear and tablecloths and so many other beautiful articles.

I had a very nice reception from the women. They were very happy to see me and kissed me – they had never met a customer from Australia before. They very rarely saw any customers because everything they produced went through the state-owned firm. They were amazed I spoke such good Hungarian. I told them that I had a Hungarian husband and that's why I could speak so well. I gave Eva a big order, on the condition that I was to be the sole distributor in Australia. She agreed and the next day I got the written agreement. After that we went to another small village, Kalocsa, where I put in another big order and another agreement was written. I was starting to become more comfortable speaking Hungarian.

I also decided I would like to import and distribute

Greta in Kalocsa peasant costume, coming home after her first buying trip to Hungary.

Herend porcelain. It was exported by a big firm called Artex. This work, which began manufacture in 1826, was unknown in Australia. It was not easy to convince the management that I should be the sole importer and distributor in Australia. They had never had any enquiries before from Australia. But I thought, so many Hungarians are coming to Australia that there will be a demand for this beautiful porcelain. The manager of Artex agreed to take me down to Herend to visit the factory. The saleslady was not very pleasant and really rather arrogant and wanted to show me that I really don't know anything about porcelain. I remember what I had read in Dale Carnegie's book *How To Win Friends and Influence People* and I used all my so-called Viennese charm to win her over. In the end she became quite friendly!

At Herend I walked round the large and impressive site, watching how they formed and hand-painted the porcelain. Everyone was very friendly and the director invited me to stay for lunch, where I enjoyed the food and the company. I placed a big order there before I left. In Budapest I talked to the general manager of Artex company and everything was arranged, though it was not very easy to convince him that I was the right person for this job. He wondered why I would import figurines, but in fact they turned out to be our best sellers.

On 21 June 1983 I received a beautiful present – a large plate – 'Presented by the Herend manufactury to Mrs Greta Rado in token of our appreciation of her work done for Herend'.

We were starting just at the right time to import and distribute these goods, especially the embroidered blouses. The 'ethnic look' was just becoming popular and we were given very much good publicity with articles and interviews in the Sydney papers. I was astonished how much publicity we got. Our best sellers were always the beautiful hand-embroidered blouses – we could never get enough of these in stock. I smiled when I saw young girls and ladies wearing them, they looked so nice. We opened a small boutique in the Cosmopolitan Arcade in Double Bay, and a big Melbourne store, Buckley and Nunn, opened a 'Hungarian Rhapsody' boutique. I myself also arranged exhibitions in Melbourne, Adelaide and Brisbane.

In 1965, I began to import beautiful figurines from the famous artist Kovacs Margit. I was very proud to be invited to her home in Budapest, where she introduced her mother as her assistant. After my first order arrived, I wanted to order more, but I was told, 'Kovacs Margit's figurines are not for export any more.' Her work is now held in a museum in Szentendre in Hungary.

Greta's Globe book catalogue.

By now we were in our new quarters at 702 George Street, near the corner of Goulburn Street. It was a large shop with a big storeroom downstairs and an office out the back. We sold Hungarian books, records, porcelain, pottery, handwoven rugs and handicrafts. On the left was the entrance to the travel agency: Andy overlooked this side of the business. I was the saleswoman and buyer and I travelled to Hungary every year. I enjoyed my stays in Budapest and I met some very nice friends . As it was always a very quick visit racing from one place to the other, I was called 'Mrs Tornado'. While I was there I had to pretend not to be too enthusiastic, or they would put up the prices!

Part Six

Besides our import business we now ran Globe International Travel Service, specialising in travel to Europe. On 1 October 1982 I was honoured with a silver medal from the official body, Austrian Tourism, Vienna. From Lufthansa we got a turbine blade from a Lufthansa Boeing 747 'In appreciation for the outstanding contribution for many years by Globe International Travel Service to Lufthansa Australia'. I was top-selling agent for Lufthansa for many years.

When we started our travel agency, air travel was so expensive that people who wanted to travel to Europe could only afford to go by boat. I loved ship travel but it took up so much of my time. But I couldn't resist the invitation from Lloyd Triestino to take part in their first crossing of the Pacific on the beautiful ocean liner *Marconi*, in February 1968. I spent my forty-seventh birthday at sea, with a celebration by the captain and friends. It was a wonderful voyage. First Suva, then Tahiti, Acapulco, across the Panama Canal to Jamaica, then over the Atlantic to Europe.

In Paris, I was so happy to see Susi, who was studying at the Sorbonne. It was the first time that she had been away from us and she missed us very much. My sister Marta, and her French husband and three sons, lived in Paris.

How Marta came to live in Paris, that's a story by itself. After the war she wanted us to go together to Australia but I was just married and awaiting the birth of my baby.

My father bought her the ticket for the ship. When it was the day she should have left Marseilles for Australia, ten people couldn't get on the ship because their berths were double-booked. The company took them back to Paris, paid for their hotel and they had to wait six weeks for the next passage to Australia. My sister, who is rather a courageous girl, decided she would go to a 'five-o'clock tea'. There she met a very handsome Frenchman, who asked her for a dance and then for another dance. Then they met nearly every day. After three weeks she told him, 'Tomorrow I will travel to Marseilles to catch the boat to Australia.' Then he asked her to marry him and of course she said yes. She rang my parents and told them, 'I'm not going to Australia, I'm staying in Paris and will get married.' I got the news on my birthday, 8 February, having had a beautiful little baby prematurely two days earlier.

1968 was not the best year to be in Paris. There was the student revolution: troops used tear gas near the Sorbonne. And there were general strikes, with no gas or electricity. We were very worried about Susi. After the troubles died down, she wanted to visit Budapest, where she was born, and also Vienna. She bought a ticket on the new jet-boat travelling up the Danube. But two days earlier came the USSR-led invasion of Czechoslovakia. People were afraid and everyone cancelled their trip to Hungary. But Susi said, 'I will still go.' The boat was nearly empty. A very nice lady started to talk to Susi and after she heard her name she said, 'Oh, I know your mother very well.' She was the general manager of Ibuz, the Hungarian state-owned travel company.

In Budapest, Susi met my cousin, who invited her to stay with them and their two daughters and showed her round the city: the house where she was born and the Spanish House where we survived the last weeks of 1944. Susi loved Budapest; she loved the walk along the Danube and up the hill to the castle, with a beautiful panorama of the city below. Everyone was astonished at how well she spoke Hungarian.

What a happy day it was for us when she came home, to see her in good health. She went straight to her balcony, admiring the beautiful view of the harbour. Soon she got a job at Sydney University teaching French.

We were very busy in our shop. I couldn't have done it without Andy. I enjoyed my trips to Hungary and Vienna, where I stayed in the nicest hotels: The Hotel Imperial, the Hotel Bristol and the Hotel Sacher, near the Opera. I never dreamt as a child that I would stay there. In the café there you can order the famous Sacher Torte. My mother's sister-in-law, Rosa, lived two minutes from the hotel and every afternoon for fifty years she went to the coffee house at the the hotel and the waiter kept the best table for her. When I was in Vienna I always knew where to find her! Rosa was 102 when she died three years ago and there is a page about her in the little book which tells the story of the hotel.

In the summer my favourite place outside the city was the health resort of Baden by Wien, one of the favourite places of the Emperor Franz Josef. Every day in the cool of the afternoon there was a concert. In the evenings we went to the wine gardens in the hills around Baden, where we could drink the new season's wine. I stayed there at the

Greta and Andy's 50th wedding anniverseary, Baden, near Vienna.

same hotel, Guttenbrunn, where Beethoven had stayed! The manageress, Hermi, became my very close friend and in 1996 she arranged our fiftieth wedding anniversary, with friends coming from all round the world, as well as the mayor of Baden and friends from Austrian Tourism. My sister Marta came from Paris with her son Gerard and daughter-in-law Lesley, cousin Eva and husband Bill from London, cousin Paul and wife Gerda from Vienna, and my cousin Robert from Vienna, who was a popular TV announcer and presenter. From Baden my old friend Elfie came, and Helga and Godfried. And from Sydney, old friends who entertained us with singing and with stories about Greta and Andy and little Susi coming to Australia. Another friend, Hansi, filmed

Greta and her cousin, Hansi, at the Goldschmieds' home in Vienna,
9 Mühlgasse, next to the coffee shop.

the whole ceremony for us. It was a beautiful wedding anniversary. We had never had a party for our wedding, so this event was a very special occasion.

My other favourite place was Bad Hofgastein near Salzburg, 890 metres up in the Alps, where we stayed at the Grand Park Hotel. Every year for twenty-five years we stayed there for a month. Our friends Hilda and Eddie from Salzburg also came there every year. Other friends we made there were Inge and Gunther from Stuttgart, who also came

Susi, Mosman, 1964.

to Sydney to see us, and Resi and Artur from Frankfurt. Resi didn't want to come back every year but Artur always came, and he played the piano for us. The hotel also had a pianist who played every night my favourite songs. Then there was Gertha, who came from Vienna but who lived in Panama from 1938. Gertha loved the old songs from the 1930s. We were called 'The Dolly Sisters' because we sang together. Sometimes we went up the mountains by cable car to 2,500 metres and we could see all the mountains covered by snow. We had such a happy time.

Back in Sydney, work was busy and we were invited to so many functions and made many good friends. I loved to go out and meet people but Andy preferred to stay at home with me. He is a very intelligent but very quiet man. Perhaps that was the success of our marriage – he never wanted to change me, he always let me be myself. In business we were a good partnership. I was always good at public relations and Andy, a born mathematician, kept everything tight and in order.

Susi had married in 1970. She met Allan at a function at the NSW Art Gallery. They fell in love and were married on 10 January 1970. Their wedding and the reception were at our place, in the garden. I hoped it wouldn't rain and we were lucky, the rain held off till all the guests had left. On 28 January 1977 Susi gave birth to a darling little girl, Linda, and on 1 July 1980, Elizabeth was born six weeks prematurely. We were very happy to have two such sweet granddaughters, who became two beautiful and clever girls. When Elizabeth was eight and Linda was eleven and a half, we invited them to come to Austria for several weeks with their mother. They enjoyed sightseeing and met my relations. After Austria, Susi took them to Germany, where they stayed with Susi's old schoolfriend, Denise, who is now a doctor and lives at Darmstadt. Her two girls were much the same age as my granddaughters.

Life seemed so good until we got the terrible news that our darling Susi had breast cancer. She had the operation and tried to be strong and hopeful. She still went to work: she was teaching French and German at Pymble Ladies College. She had her chemotherapy on weekends so that she would not miss work. Chemotherapy was still so primitive and breast cancer was a dangerous disease. I believe that if she had got cancer now she would have survived it.

In June 1991 we had been married for forty-five years. We bought a first-class ticket for Susi to join us in Austria. We

Greta and Susi, Vienna, 1991.

met her at Frankfurt airport then went to our favourite hotel
at Baden. We also went together to Vienna and I showed her
all my favourite places where I walked as a little girl. My
friend, Hansi, offered to take us down to Lake Neusiedler See,
which we crossed on our escape in 1948. The gypsy huts at

Moerbisch are gone: it is now an elegant summer resort with an open-air theatre on the lake. I tried to find the place where we came ashore on that cold November afternoon but it was impossible – it had changed so much. I told Susi about the difficult seven hours we had spent on the boat.

Susi wanted to see Budapest with a Hungarian taxi whose driver knew the quickest way. We started at Baden and then went to the village where my grandparents had lived. From there we went to Budapest. We visited the house where we used to live, which became the Swedish House, and where so many people were rounded up the night on the 31 December 1944 and killed and shot in the Danube at St Istvan Park. Susi wanted to see once more the house at 38 St Istvan Park (the Spanish House) where we were so lucky to survive this dangerous time.

After three days we caught a taxi back to Baden and stayed at the the Hotel Guttenbrunn. From there we went by car five hours to Bad Hofgastein where we stayed two weeks with Susi. She met our friends, who all came like us every year at this time. Susi joined every day a walking group – she wanted to walk everywhere. Maybe she had the feeling that later on she would not be able to walk.

Some days after she arrived in Sydney we had a call that the cancer had spread to her bones. We returned to Sydney. Susi still tried to be strong but on 3 December 1992 she lost her fight with cancer. It was a great loss to all of us: to Allan, Linda and Elizabeth, to Andy and me. There is a saying, 'Children have to bury their parents but parents should never have to bury their children.' Susi brought sunshine into all our lives. In an obituary written for the school magazine, a

Linda and Elizabeth's graduation, Macquarie University, 2003.

teacher from Pymble Ladies College called her 'a queen among women'.

It has been a long time ago but there is not a day when I don't think about our darling Susi. I'm sad that she couldn't enjoy seeing her two daughters growing up. Both girls went to Macquarie University: Linda got a Masters degree in science and Elizabeth finished her science studies with first class honours. As the girls grew up they became closer to Andy and me and I feel that they are now my closest friends.

On 10 December 1999, Linda and Luke were married. It was a beautiful wedding but I was sad that Susi couldn't see it. Linda and Luke now live in Hobart. I miss Linda but we have long chats on the telephone. Elizabeth has a good job as a scientist with a big firm in Sydney. She took a year's unpaid holiday to go round Australia with her friend Duane and go climbing mountains in South America.

In 2001, Andy and I were married fifty-five years and decided to have a little party at the Grand Park Hotel in Bad Hofgastein. We invited our close friends again and our granddaughters and Linda's husband Luke. It was a very nice party with lots of speeches! Suddenly Elizabeth came up

Linda and Elizabeth, Venice, 2001.

and spoke so cleverly…she had some funny remarks about her grandmother! My friend Alois played the cymbalon and Artur played the piano.

Our grandaughters and Luke loved the mountains and the life in this little country town. After ten days I took them by car to Vienna. I showed them the house where I lived for nearly eighteen years after I was born, and also my school. Without any knowledge of German they walked everywhere and managed to see so much! One evening I took them to the outskirts of Vienna where a friend who used to be the manager of the Austrian Tourism invited us to a famous Heurigen or wine cellar. Linda and Elizabeth were amazed to see Nana drinking wine out of a big beer glass! Before they went home, Luke and the girls presented me with an album of all the photos they had taken that day, with such clever captions.

Greta and Andy, Mosman, on Greta's 85th birthday.

Now we felt we did not want to work so much any more and we sold our business. After Andy was ninety-one, he didn't like to travel any more. I still went overseas but I missed him so much that I always came back early. Dr. David Farbenblum, who has been our doctor for twenty-two years knew that I couldn't manage Andy on my own, especially after I had an aortic aneurism operation eleven years ago. Dr. Ian Fielding told me that he found that aneurism by a lucky coincidence when he operated on me for breast cancer. Now I had to see Professor Appleberg, who operated successfully at the last minute. He told me never to lift anything heavy. Now that I couldn't help Andy I looked around and found a nursing home, Amity Grand, in Mosman, three minutes drive from our home. It is very comfortable and luxurious but still, it wasn't Andy's home. Two very nice ladies there, Michelle Megson and Grescha Brewer, are very helpful to us.

It is very difficult after sixty-one years of a happy marriage not to be together any more. I visit him nearly every day and he says, 'I love you, Greta.'

Susi adored her father. The last words she wrote in hospital were 'When will I start my mother's story?' She wasn't able to write any more. Now, I try to fulfil her wish and I am writing my story for Linda and Elizabeth.

Appendix One: Giorgio Perlasca

Giorgio Perlasca, an Italian who had fought for Franco in Spain, later saved more than 5,000 Jewish families from the Hungarian Nazis. Perlasca left Spain in 1938 with a letter from the Spanish authorities saying they would help him wherever he might be in the world. On arrival in Hungary he went to the Spanish Consulate and showed them the letter. Here he was given a passport and assumed the name Jorge Perlasca. Here he also learned that Spain was providing 'letters of protection' for Hungarian Jews, who were now obliged to wear a yellow star. Spain had eight apartment blocks in Budapest where they accommodated Jews under Spanish protection.

Perlasca offered to help with this program. On arrival at the consulate one morning in 1944, Perlasca found that the Consul had fled to Switzerland – he was now the only person there with a Spanish passport. By this time it was impossible to communicate with Madrid and the assistance program for Jews was in jeopardy. In order to save the program Perlasca went to the Ministry of Foreign Affairs and convinced officials that he had been made the Spanish Consul. He proceeded to give consular letters of protection to whoever requested them. He organised food, medical aid and protection for 5,200 Jewish families in the consulate apartment blocks. He had various informants who would let him know when to intervene and fend off attempted Nazi searches of the apartments.

On 16 January 1945 the Red Army entered Budapest and the Jews in the protected apartment blocks were now free to leave. Perlasca, as a consul of a Fascist government, had to flee the country and eventually moved to Italy.

In 1989 the Hungarian Parliament awarded him its major honour, while Israel gave him honorary citizenship.

Only 200,000 of Hungary's 750,000 Jews survived the war. It is to this man, Giorgio Perlasca, that Greta and her father, mother and sister owe their survival.

Appendix Two: Raoul Wallenberg

Wallenberg, a Swedish diplomat, is estimated to have rescued tens of thousands of Hungarian Jews during the Holocaust.

Raoul Wallenberg was a member of one of Sweden's most prominent families. The Wallenbergs have given their country several generations of leading bankers, diplomats and statesmen. Raoul's father, Raoul Oscar Wallenberg, was a naval officer but died three months before his son was born.

Raoul was born on 4 August 1912, and his grandfather, Gustav Wallenberg, took charge of Raoul's education. The plan was that he would follow the family tradition and go into banking, but he turned out to be more interested in architecture and trade. After compulsory military service he studied architecture and in 1935 received a Bachelor of Science degree.

Because Wallenberg had a good feeling for languages and could travel freely around Europe he came in contact with some Hungarian business partners. By late June 1944 Raoul Wallenberg had been appointed first secretary of the Swedish diplomatic mission in Budapest. But this was no normal diplomatic posting. His brief was to initiate a rescue mission for the Jews.

After the German occupation of Hungary on 19 March 1944, Jews were rounded up from the countryside and deported. The deportation trains carried them to Auschwitz and Birkenau where certain death awaited them.

In desperation, many Jewish inhabitants of Budapest sought help from the embassies of neutral states, including Sweden. The embassies issued temporary passports to Jews who had special ties with these countries.

Raoul Wallenberg's first task was to design a Swedish protective passport to help the Jews in their dealings with the Germans and the Hungarians. At first he only had permission to issue 1,500 such passports, but he managed to persuade the Hungarian authorities to let him issue another 1,000; he eventually managed to get the quota raised to 4,500. In reality he managed to issue more than three times this number. His staff, all Jews under his protection, grew to several hundred people.

Now Wallenberg began to expand the 'Swedish houses'. These were more than thirty buildings in the Pest district where Jews could seek shelter. The number in these 'Swedish houses' soon climbed to 15,000.

On October 15 the Hungarian government was replaced by the leader of the Hungarian Nazis, Ferenc Szalasi. He was the leader of the Arrow Cross movement, which was feared at least as much as the German Nazis for its cruel methods in dealing with the Jews. Now the brutal death marches started. Thousands of Jews marched in endless columns along the 200-kilometre route between Budapest and the Austrian border. Raoul Wallenberg stayed with them continuously, distributing food and medicine and alternately theatening and bribing the Nazis until he managed to secure the release of those with Swedish passports.

The arrival of the Soviet troops in January 1945 meant an end to these deportations. But Raoul Wallenberg disappeared. Was he killed by Russian soldiers? Or taken prisoner and taken to the Soviet Union? If he did become a lifelong prisoner in Russia, as much evidence suggests, it was a cruel and ironic fate for a man who devoted his life to securing freedom for thousands of his fellow human beings. According to Per Anger, his friend and colleague, Wallenberg must be given credit for having saved about 100,000 Jews.

For further reading, see John Bierman, *Righteous Gentile: the story of Raoul Wallenberg, missing hero of the Holocaust*, Viking Press, New York, 1981.

Acknowledgements

I am grateful to all the nice people who have been so kind to my husband and myself.

To my two granddaughters, Linda and Elizabeth.

To my friends and family in Sydney and Europe.

To the management, staff, nurses and carers of Amity Grand of Mosman.

To the Swedish Consulate in Sydney for their help with the story of Raoul Wallenberg.

And my sincere thanks to Jenny Horsfield; without her help and encouragement I could have never written this book.

Greta Rado
Sydney, 8 February 2008